Arts: A Third Level Course

The Nineteenth-century Novel and its Legacy Unit 4

A Study Guide to Wuthering Heights

Prepared by Graham Holderness for the Course Team

The Open University Press

Graham Holderness, formerly Research Assistant in The Open University, is Lecturer in English at University College, Swansea.

The Open University Press
Walton Hall, Bletchley, Bucks.

First published 1973.

Designed by the Media Development Group of the Open University.

Printed in Great Britain by
Martin Cadbury Printing Group

SBN 335 00813 5

This text forms part of the correspondence element of an Open University Third Level Course The complete list of units in the course is given at the end of this text.

For general availability of supporting material referred to in this text, please write to the Director of Marketing, The Open University, Walton Hall, Bletchley, Bucks.

Further information on Open University courses may be obtained from the Admissions Office, The Open University, P.O. Box 48, Bletchley, Bucks.

CONTENTS

Introduction

The Study Guide to *Wuthering Heights* is divided into two parts: *Part One* is the Guide proper; *Part Two* is a collection of information about the novel and the novelist. The information about the novel (Part Two, Sections 1, 2, 3) will be of use to you only after you have completed your reading of *Wuthering Heights.*

1 The purpose of this Study Guide is to provide you with an approach to *Wuthering Heights.* Some guided reading is given of certain passages in the earlier part of the novel: but the main emphasis in the Guide is on questions which are designed to direct your attention to the important problems, and to make you think about them. There are two types of question: (a) specific questions, which I want you to attempt as you go through the Guide (the way you do it is up to you; I suggest that you map out specimen answers in the form of notes); and (b) more general questions which I'd like you to bear in mind as you read the novel. All the questions will be answered, and the issues they raise discussed, in Unit 5.

Wuthering Heights has been subjected to a wide variety of interpretation by literary critics. For this reason I have tried to avoid arguing strongly in the Study Guide for any one view of what it is really about, what kind of a novel it is: I have preferred to present you with conflicting interpretations which you can then check against your own responses. I want above all to avoid pre-empting your personal experience of the novel.

2 The Study Guide restricts its references to the first nine chapters of *Wuthering Heights*; and should be read in conjunction with these. Although it looks forward to the rest of the book, the Guide *assumes* specific acquaintance only with the first 130 pages. All page references are to the Penguin English Library edition, edited by David Daiches (1965). (It is important that you should read this text rather than any other: the reasons for this are given in Part Two, Section 3.)

On page 16 of the Penguin edition you will find a genealogical table and a time-chart, which you will probably find useful, if you get confused about relationships or chronological sequence. Another possible source of confusion is the two Catherines—precisely which one is being referred to. To avoid this, I have called the first Catherine (Heathcliff's) *Catherine,* throughout; and her daughter, *Cathy.* (This is an arbitrary choice, and doesn't follow the novel. There Heathcliff calls Catherine Cathy, and Edgar calls her Catherine.)

3 One of the big differences between *Wuthering Heights* and *Mansfield Park* is that *Wuthering Heights* has a much more complicated and highly organized structure. The story is not explicitly told by the author herself, or even by a narrator who reflects or represents the author's view, like *Mansfield Park* or *Middlemarch*: it is instead a series of personal narratives: every word in the book is spoken by one of the characters involved in the action, and the author never makes her presence directly felt. I think this narrative technique is important in the novel, and that's where I propose to begin.

There are two broadcast programmes associated with this unit, one television and one radio. The television programme is intended to suggest something of Emily Brontë's life at Haworth; and also to try to explain how her imagination worked. The radio broadcast is by Raymond Williams: "The Nature of Wuthering Heights."

I would like to thank particularly Arnold Kettle, Graham Martin and John Purkis for their helpful and stimulating comments and suggestions.

Emily Brontë by P. B. Brontë
(National Portrait Gallery)

PART ONE

1 NARRATIVE TECHNIQUE

In this section I will be considering the role of Lockwood in the first two chapters: but first read Chapters One and Two, paying particular attention to Lockwood the narrator.

The narrator, who is to introduce himself as Mr Lockwood, is very much there: 'I' is the first word in the novel. If we can deduce from the opening of *Mansfield Park* that Jane Austen is first producing an 'objective' social setting within which her tale is to operate, we get from *Wuthering Heights*, through the immediate introduction of an 'I' a sense that everything in this book is likely to proceed through personal impression, experience refracted, so to speak, through the mind of one of the characters.[1]

This paragraph from Unit 1 introduces our first major topic: the narrative technique of *Wuthering Heights*. In Unit 1 Arnold Kettle pointed out a basic difference between *Mansfield Park* and *Wuthering Heights*. Jane Austen's novel 'establishes an immensely solid sense of social reality' and also 'a way of looking at this social scene which is *familiar* yet critical'. The opening of *Wuthering Heights*, by contrast, faces the reader with 'a situation in which he can be sure of nothing'. In this first paragraph, Unit 1 goes on, words are brought together which aren't naturally associated: 'Solitary/neighbour'; 'misanthropists/Heaven'; 'my heart warmed towards him when I beheld his black eyes withdraw'. I agree that the effect of these juxtapositions is to disorientate the reader and assault his complacency. But they also have a more specific function, which is to tell us what kind of a man Lockwood is. And as you will see, this is something Emily Brontë wants us to be aware of.

It appears that Lockwood is on the run from an abortive love-affair in Brighton or some other fashionable coastal resort (pages 47–8). The experience is described on page 48 in the paragraph beginning: 'While enjoying a month of fine weather at the sea-coast . . .'

Exercise

Look carefully at the language of that paragraph. Underline the words and phrases which could be described as clichés, or artificial. What kind of a man would you imagine talking like that?

Specimen Answer

These are the phrases I would have underlined: 'a most fascinating creature'; 'a real goddess'; 'I never told my love'; 'head over ears'; 'persuaded her mamma to decamp'. The language is very artificial, riddled with clichés and conventional phrases; it suggests a superficial and frivolous kind of man, perhaps a fashionable Regency dandy. (Lockwood is probably a fairly ordinary kind of man affecting fashionable manners.) Can you imagine Heathcliff or Cathy or Joseph 'enjoying a month of fine weather at the sea-coast'?

[1] A302, *The Nineteenth Century Novel and its Legacy*, Unit 1 *Introduction*, p. 18.

Lockwood reveals, by the language he uses, the difference between himself and the people he is visiting. Now what about the experience itself? He describes how he approached close to a relationship with a woman; but as soon as he realized that the connection was developing beyond the level of flirtation (i.e. the social reflection of a relationship without any real interchange of feeling) he bolted. Lockwood has been confronted with the fact of passion, love, relationship; and he has shrunk away from it. In Part One, Section 4.3, I talk about the love between Catherine and Heathcliff, which is probably the major theme of the novel. As you read the novel it will become clear that Lockwood's shying away from passion is intended as a contrast with the love of Catherine and Heathcliff. (Later on, a similar contrast is made between Heathcliff and Edgar Linton.) It develops further the difference between Lockwood, and the world of the Heights.

Lockwood then goes into an affected misanthropist's retreat in faraway Yorkshire, pretending to isolate himself from society like a Byronic hero, brooding over a hidden sorrow. That's how he sees himself, anyway. But he still remains the genteel city-dweller, pleasantly companionable, anxious to be on friendly terms with his neighbours. 'It is astonishing how sociable I feel myself compared with him' (page 50). He can't understand why at the Heights nobody utters 'a word of sociable conversation' (page 56); and when nobody will admit him to the house he imagines 'perpetual isolation from your species' (page 51) to be the worst possible kind of punishment.

The meeting between Lockwood and Heathcliff is a collision of two different and distinct social worlds: an independent, sociable city-dweller is introduced to a remote Yorkshire farmhouse where nothing is as he expects it to be. So naturally he begins to make mistakes. His first *faux pas* is to mistake Heathcliff for what he himself is—an ordinary upper-class gentleman pretending to be a recluse—a dilettante misanthropist: 'I felt interested in a man who seemed more *exaggeratedly reserved* than myself' (page 45; my italics). 'Exaggeratedly reserved'—Lockwood implies that Heathcliff is putting it on, as he is, rather than demonstrating a *natural* reserve.

Between pages 52 and 56 Lockwood makes a series of mistakes about the Heights and its people, each one getting him deeper and deeper into misapprehension. He compliments Cathy on her 'favourites', only to discover that they are dead rabbits. He assumes that Cathy will be as amiable and hospitable as the ladies of his own social milieu: but is swiftly disillusioned when she flings the teaspoon back into the caddy. He takes Hareton to be a servant or common labourer because of his dress and manner; and gets entirely the wrong idea about the system of relationships at the Heights.

Read through those pages now (52–56) and consider the following questions about Lockwood's function as narrator. I'd like you to draft answers to (a), (b) and (c), and leave (d) for further consideration. I will discuss them all further in Unit 5.

(a) What do these pages tell us about Lockwood?

(b) What do they tell us about the Heights and the people who live there?

(c) What do you think was Emily Brontë's purpose, in arriving at her subject through the intermediary of Lockwood, as narrator of the first part of the story?

Lockwood narrates for the first three chapters. Then Nelly Dean (the servant alternatively of the Earnshaws and the Lintons) takes over and she is narrator for the remainder of the novel, as she tells the story to Lockwood. She is interrupted only by Heathcliff's account of the visit to Thrushcross Grange (pp. 88–92); two passages from Isabella Linton, a letter (173–182) and a longer passage of narrative (208–218); and a short passage of narrative from another servant, Zillah (323–328). These will be discussed in Unit 5. The big question to bear in mind as you read *Wuthering Heights* is this:

(d) Why does Emily Brontë use the device of a narrator to present her story? Does it make much difference—is it merely a convenient literary device, or does it make a real contribution to our experience of the novel?

Some critics (those for example who think that *Wuthering Heights* is a transcendental novel) believe that the function of Lockwood and Nelly is to reveal the inadequacy of empirical, commonsense judgement when confronted with the reality of spiritual experience. So that when Nelly tries to explain away spiritual happenings, she is showing how little of experience she really understands:

> Everything is contained in the mind of Lockwood, who begins the novel with his curious poking about the Heights, . . . trying to understand and interpret what he sees. Nelly is like Lockwood, both in her need to understand and in having staked her comprehension of life on the objective level of empirical reality. She lives in a world of things and of rational, causal explanations of events: here she is secure, in control, and is being rewarded for her control. Anything not reducible to this level of existence is, for both Lockwood and Nelly, a threat to their hold on reality.[1]

You can see straightaway from this quotation that your view of the narrative technique will be determined by your view of what the novel is about. On the other hand, Arnold Kettle attaches more value to the rationalism and 'normality' of Nelly Dean: he thinks that it helps to keep the novel close to the ground and believable (though with the qualification that rationality is at least partly inadequate):

> The roles of the two narrators, Lockwood and Nelly Dean, are not casual. Their function (they are the two most 'normal' people in the book) is partly to keep the story close to the earth, to make it believable, partly to comment on it from a common-sense point of view and thereby to reveal in part the inadequacy of such common sense. They act as a kind of sieve to the story, sometimes a double sieve, which has the purpose not simply of separating off the chaff, but of making us aware of the difficulty of passing easy judgements.[2]

The only other point I want to make in this section is this. In Part Two, Section 4 of the Guide you will read about Emily Brontë's life; how different it was from the 'normal' urban middle-class life of the time—that of people like Lockwood. The life at Wuthering Heights which is so unfamiliar to Lockwood is not unfamiliar at all to Emily Brontë. As you will see in the television programme, there were striking similarities between her life at Haworth Parsonage and the kind of life depicted at the Heights. Here are two passages which describe the peculiarities of Yorkshire people, and suggest how unsettling it could be for a southern city-dweller to meet them. The first is from Mrs

[1] Thomas A. Vogler (ed.) *Twentieth Century Interpretations of Wuthering Heights*, Prentice-Hall, 1968.
[2] Arnold Kettle, *An Introduction to the English Novel*, vol. 1, Hutchinson, 1951.

Gaskell's *Life of Charlotte Brontë* (1858); the second was written in 1946 by V. S. Pritchett.

Even an inhabitant of the neighbouring county of Lancashire is struck by the peculiar force of character which the Yorkshiremen display . . . the remarkable degree of self-sufficiency they possess gives them an air of independence rather apt to repel a stranger.

[The Yorkshireman] belongs to that keen, yet short-sighted class who consider suspicion of all whose honesty is not proved a sign of wisdom.

Their affections are strong, and their foundations lie deep: but they are not widespreading; nor do they show themselves on the surface. . . . Their accost is curt; their accent and tone of speech blunt and harsh. . . . Their feelings are not easily aroused, but their duration is lasting.[1]

Wuthering Heights is a poetic novel: but it seems to me the most realistic statement about the Yorkshire people of the isolated moorland and dales that I have ever read. I am a southerner, but I spent a good deal of my childhood in those Northern cottages, and I recognise the implacable belligerent people of Emily Brontë's novel at once. . . . Austere, empty and ominous were the earth and sky, and the air was fiercer and more violent than in the South. The occasional small stone houses stuck up like forts, the people themselves seemed, to a southerner, as stern as soldiers, and even the common sentences they spoke were so turned that, but for a quizzical glitter in the eyes of the speaker, one might have taken their words as a challenge, insult or derision. I do not mean that these remote Yorkshire people were not kindly and hospitable folk; but one had not to live among them for long, before one found that their egotism was naked, their hatred unending. They seemed to revel in a hostility, which they called frankness or bluntness.[2]

2 HEATHCLIFF

'Heathcliff is the hero of the book, if hero there be . . .'

Heathcliff is really the central problem of *Wuthering Heights*: our valuation of him determines our sense of what the novel is about. If you think about it, it would perhaps be more orthodox to regard Edgar Linton —who has all the conventional requirements—as the hero, and Heathcliff as the villain of the piece. Heathcliff never does anything virtuous or noble in the conventional sense: his story is a long list of morally reprehensible actions. Are we supposed to see Heathcliff for what he is—'an incarnation of evil qualities; implacable hate, ingratitude, cruelty, falsehood, selfishness, and revenge'— and despise it? Or are we supposed to sympathize with him in his obsessive pursuit of love and then revenge?

In Part Two, Section 2, which deals with contemporary responses to the novel, you will read that in the 1840s critics were divided on the subject of the book's 'morality'. Those who thought the book *immoral* seem to have assumed that Emily Brontë wanted us to admire the obviously immoral Heathcliff. Those who

[1] Elizabeth Gaskell, *Life of Charlotte Brontë* (1858), World's Classics, Oxford University Press, 1919,
[2] V. S. Pritchett, 'Implacable, Belligerent People of Wuthering Heights', *New Statesman*, xxi, 22 June. 1946. Reprinted by permission.

thought it moral assumed that she wanted us to judge him. These two ways of looking at him aren't the only ones; but they are the most common. How then are we supposed to see Heathcliff?

If we look at what he actually does in the novel, in the abstract, it's a pretty disgusting performance. This process is attempted in a critical article by Philip Drew called 'Charlotte Brontë as a Critic of *Wuthering Heights*'[1]. Drew thinks that Charlotte Brontë ('Heathcliff never swerves from his arrowstraight course to perdition') was right about Heathcliff. When she tackled the problem of orientation within the moral world of the novel—the problem of knowing what we should think, what we should feel, how we should value—she solved the problem by reading it firmly within a known and recognizable moral system.[2]

Charlotte's assessment of Heathcliff depends on a recognition of his superhuman villainy, whereas modern critics . . . usually choose to minimise or justify Heathcliff's consistent delight in malice in order to elevate him to the status of a hero.

Drew then provides a long catalogue or charge-sheet of Heathcliff's actual misdemeanours. Catherine calls him 'a pitiless, wolvish man', and this assessment is borne out by his actions. When he returns to Wuthering Heights as an adult, he immediately begins to lead Hindley Earnshaw to perdition; he courts Isabella Linton not out of love but desire for revenge; he breaks up the marriage between Catherine and Edgar; he has a fight with Hindley in which he knocks him down and kicks him; there is evidence that he murdered Hindley; he degrades and perverts Hareton; he treats his own son Linton with great cruelty, traps the second Cathy into marrying him, and finally lets him die without calling a doctor. All these actions are perpetrated with a savage and voracious appetite for inflicting cruelty. Drew sums up:

His whole career is one of calculated malice: during this time he does not perform one good or kindly action, and continually expresses his hatred of all the other characters. So extreme is his malevolence that one might expect him to impress critics as a grotesque villain like Quilp in the *Old Curiosity Shop*.

What Drew does here is to abstract incidents from the novel so as to bring them under the contemplation of our normal moral consciousness, the conventional social morality with which we generally approach everyday living. But like *Great Expectations*, *Wuthering Heights* is the kind of book that attempts to create new values rather than to celebrate existing ones. It's no good saying that the novel operates within the familiar orthodox moral system, when it is trying to create its own moral universe, by means of its artistic organization.

That sounds rather abstruse and difficult, so I'll try to illustrate what I mean straight away by taking an example, again of the novel's narrative technique. Please read pages 95–96: from 'Under these circumstances I remained solitary' to 'Nelly, make me decent, I'm going to be good'.

At this point Catherine has returned from Thrushcross Grange a lady, and Hindley banishes Heathcliff from her company. We have seen Catherine's attitude to Heathcliff change at the beginning of this chapter: but then we may

[1] Philip Drew, 'Charlotte Brontë as a Critic of *Wuthering Heights*', *19th Century Fiction*, 1964. You will find it reprinted in M. Allott (ed) *Wuthering Heights, A Collection of Critical Essays*, Macmillan Casebook Series, 1970.
[2] See the 'Biographical Notice of Ellis and Acton Bell' in the Penguin edition, pp. 30–41, for Charlotte's criticism of her sister's novel.

feel that Heathcliff's banishment is perfectly natural and right. The thing is, we aren't allowed to look at the situation objectively: we are shown Nelly's feelings, which then direct our sympathy towards Heathcliff in his position as outcast. We aren't free as readers to judge objectively: the author directs our judgements for us. Notice also that Heathcliff's decision to 'be decent'—a decision arrived at through internal struggle, and motivated by his love and respect for Catherine—is in moral terms far superior to Catherine's treatment of him.

I'd like to leave Heathcliff at this point by referring you to a passage, and giving you some questions to think about. Please read from page 76 at the bottom ('One fine summer morning') to the end of Chapter 4. This is the passage which introduces Heathcliff into the novel, and it's an important one. Notice throughout how Heathcliff is *treated* by the people around him. Notice especially this section (my italics):

Miss Cathy and he were now very thick; but Hindley *hated* him, and to say the truth I did the same; and we *plagued* and went on with him shamefully, for I wasn't reasonable enough to feel my *injustice*, and the mistress never put in a word on his behalf, when she saw him *wronged*.

He seemed a sullen, patient child; *hardened*, perhaps to ill-treatment: he would stand Hindley's blows without winking or shedding a tear, and my pinches moved him only to draw in a breath, and open his eyes as if he had hurt himself by accident, and nobody was to blame.

This endurance made old Earnshaw furious when he discovered his son *persecuting* the poor, fatherless child, as he called him.

Exercise

Write a short answer, in note form, to the following question: Read the incident in which Heathcliff forces Hindley to exchange horses. What do you think this incident is designed to tell us about Heathcliff?

As you read through the novel, consider the following questions:

(a) Does your knowledge of the way Heathcliff is *treated* (by Hindley, by Edgar, by Catherine) help you to *understand* his behaviour? Does it *justify* it?

(b) At any given point, do you sympathize with Heathcliff, or feel objectively critical? (Be careful to take into account the attitude of whoever is telling the story.)

(c) Can you believe in Heathcliff as a human being?

3 THE LANGUAGE OF WUTHERING HEIGHTS

We have already examined one example of the novel's use of language: Lockwood's account of his experience by the sea (p. 48). I will now ask you to look at some more examples, and to think about the way Emily Brontë uses language, and to what purposes she puts different kinds of language.

3.1 Narrative prose

On that bleak hill-top the earth was hard with a black frost, and the air made me shiver through every limb. Being unable to remove the chain, I jumped over, and, running up the flagged causeway bordered with straggling gooseberry bushes, knocked vainly for admittance, till my knuckles tingled, and the dogs howled.

'Wretched inmates!' I ejaculated, mentally, 'you deserve perpetual isolation from your species for your churlish inhospitality. At least, I would not keep my doors barred in the day time—I don't care—I will get in!'

(p. 51)

Exercise

Do you notice any difference between the language of these two paragraphs?

Answer

Lockwood's speech is pompous, artificial, bookish: not really approximating to ordinary speech, or close to actual experience. By contrast the language of the first paragraph is very close to reality.

Discussion

The combination in the first paragraph of simple, vivid words like 'bleak', 'hard', 'black'; verbs of action and movement like 'shivered', 'jumped', 'running', 'knocked'; and precise descriptive details such as the 'flagged causeway bordered with straggling gooseberry bushes', 'my knuckles tingled', 'the dogs howled'—makes the whole scene come very much alive. It seems very close to real experience.

The language is of course *literary*—this 'poetic' evocation of experience is after all only a literary device, not to be confused with real experience—but the total effect resembles an experience enacted. This suggests one of the reasons why *Wuthering Heights* has been called a 'Dramatic Poem'—because of the vividness, the immediacy, the precision with which it presents its material.

So I think we could say that the kinds of language used in these two paragraphs are quite distinct: while Lockwood's speech works on an inflated rhetorical level ('wretched inmates', 'perpetual isolation') the descriptive prose presents, in a very hard-hitting way, experience—by using words which (mainly because of their use in common speech) are close to actuality.

3.2 Speech

In Unit 1 Arnold Kettle talked about this 'mixture of the colloquial and the stilted' in the speech of Emily Brontë's characters; and suggested that this might be due to 'her own unease, as a woman, in guessing exactly how men talk in the absence of women'.

Personally I think Emily Brontë was probably a good deal cleverer than that. We've seen that Lockwood reveals his character by using stilted, artificial, literary language. He almost expects people to behave as they do in books—remember how he 'warmed towards' Heathcliff when he thought he was acting the part of a misanthropist—but was shocked when Heathcliff revealed a '*genuine* bad nature'. This is how one critic puts it:

> There is something basically wrong, which is reflected in Lockwood's diction. He expects (and wants) people to behave as they do in novels; he wants life to imitate a certain kind of art in the way in which life often does when people follow conventional roles in order to structure their experience. But these are people who do not choose to behave that way, and Lockwood is as helpless and lost as the reader expecting a conventional literary experience.[1]

Of course, we can find Heathcliff using artificial speech too: the dialogue in *Wuthering Heights* is not naturalistic, except where Joseph and Hareton use dialect. Emily Brontë uses a variety of styles, and all the resources of language at her command, to say what she wants to say. Nevertheless, most of the time the language is deeply rooted in actual common experience: and this is what gives the book its precise and concrete quality.

Exercise

Look now at the passage below. Again, what differences do you notice between the first paragraph and the rest?

> ' "T' maister nobbut just buried, and Sabbath nut oer'red, und t' sahnd uh't gospel still i' yer lugs, and yah darr be laiking! shame on ye! sit ye dahn, ill childer! they's good books eneugh if ye'll read 'em; sit ye dahn, and think uh yer sowls!"
>
> 'Saying this, he compelled us to square our positions that we might receive, from the far-off fire, a dull ray to show us the text of the lumber he thrust upon us.
>
> 'I could not bear the employment. I took my dingy volume by the scroop, and hurled it into the dog-kennel, vowing I hated a good book.
>
> 'Heathcliff kicked his to the same place.
>
> 'Then there was a hubbub!'
>
> (p. 63)

Answer

A trick question, that. Obviously Joseph's dialect is different from the language Catherine uses. But isn't there a rather strong *similarity* between the dialect and Catherine's speech?

[1] Thomas A. Vogler, *op. cit.*

Discussion

Again we find strongly physical, active verbs 'square', 'hurled', 'kicked'; and expressive adjectives like 'dull' and 'dingy'. But the main thing I think is that the movement, tone, texture of Catherine's speech is that of common speech, not so very far from the dialect—'the *lumber* he *thrust* upon us'; 'I took my dingy volume by the scroop'; 'hurled it into the dog-kennel'; 'Heathcliff kicked his to the same place'; 'then there was a hubbub!'

We see and feel those actions so vividly, because of the expressive and colloquial and concrete quality of the language.

Exercise

As a final exercise, could you please look up page 77 and read the paragraph 'It seemed a long while . . . the three kingdoms'. This is part of Nelly Dean's narrative. What kind of language do you think she is using? Try and write an answer to that question, and we'll come back to it in Unit 5.

4 CATHERINE AND HEATHCLIFF

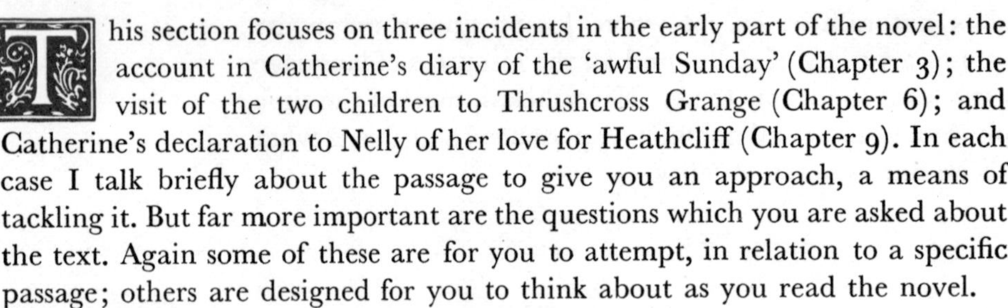

This section focuses on three incidents in the early part of the novel: the account in Catherine's diary of the 'awful Sunday' (Chapter 3); the visit of the two children to Thrushcross Grange (Chapter 6); and Catherine's declaration to Nelly of her love for Heathcliff (Chapter 9). In each case I talk briefly about the passage to give you an approach, a means of tackling it. But far more important are the questions which you are asked about the text. Again some of these are for you to attempt, in relation to a specific passage; others are designed for you to think about as you read the novel.

4.1 'An awful Sunday'

Please read pages 62–64: from 'An awful Sunday!' to 'and swears he will reduce him to his right place—'.

Catherine's diary describes the nature and quality of her early relationship with Heathcliff. When these events occur old Earnshaw is dead and Hindley is master of the Heights. We have seen already his policy of persecuting Heathcliff: in this account Catherine and Heathcliff are persecuted together—compelled to sit shivering in a garret, listening to Joseph reading sermons, while Hindley and his wife 'bask in fatuous comfort before the fire'. Their response to these conditions is to engage in a mutual rebellion against their repression.

I think this is an incident to bear in mind at later stages in the novel. The best way of focusing on it is to try and decide: what is your *valuation* of the actions of Catherine and Heathcliff? Do you see them as naughty children, defying their elders, disrupting the order of the household? Obviously they *are* that. But is that quite how you would put it?

One possible point of view is that represented by Arnold Kettle in his *Introduction to the English Novel.* He thinks that we are introduced to the love of Catherine and Heathcliff as an emotional bond forged in a mutual response to ill-treatment. Hindley's reaction to this show of resistance is to try and split Catherine and Heathcliff, by discriminating against Heathcliff on grounds of class: Hindley 'swears he will reduce him to his right place.'

Against this degradation Catherine and Heathcliff rebel, hurling their pious books into the dog-kennel. And in their revolt they discover their deep and passionate need of each other. He, the outcast slummy, turns to the lively, spirited, fearless girl who alone offers him understanding and comradeship, And she, born into the world of Wuthering Heights senses that to achieve a full humanity, to be true to herself as a human being, she must associate herself totally with him in his rebellion against the tyranny of the Earnshaws and all that tyranny involves.[1]

As a contrast to this view we can consider Dorothy van Ghent's essay in the Course Reader. She would see Catherine and Heathcliff here demonstrating their qualities of 'immoderation' and 'excess'. She thinks that *Wuthering Heights* presents to the imagination two kinds of reality: the raw, inhuman reality of anonymous natural energies; and the restrictive reality of civilized manners and habits. Catherine and Heathcliff are 'portions of the flux of nature, trying to identify themselves as human, but disrupting life by their appetite for an inhuman kind of intercourse'.

Think about it.

4.2 Thrushcross Grange

Please read Chapter 6, and Chapter 7 up to page 95—'I like to be dirty, and I will be dirty'.

In Catherine's diary she envisages taking a 'scamper on the moors'. That scamper is the visit to Thrushcross Grange described on these pages (88–92). In the first paragraph of the account 'Cathy and I escaped from the wash-house' Heathcliff recalls the details of the 'awful Sunday' to make the connection explicit.

The contrast and relationship between the two houses (the Heights and the Grange) is one of the basic structural devices binding the novel together. The relationships are generally made explicit, and I don't intend at this stage to discuss the various different ways of interpreting the contrast—I'll leave that for the Unit on the novel. Just be aware of it, and try as you are reading to sort out your own idea of what the contrast really means. I'll now go over in some detail the opening pages of Chapter 7; and then leave you to consider some questions about Chapter 6.

Take the first paragraph of Chapter 7 (p. 93). Catherine returns from her stay at the Grange very much altered, from a 'hatless little savage' to 'a very dignified person'. It has been suggested that the nature of this change is a transformation of Catherine from a child to an adult:

The first glimpse we have of them is through Cathy's eyes, on the brink of rebellion. Cathy's narrative ends with her plans for a scamper on the moor in the rain, beneath the dairy woman's cloak. It is not until Heathcliff's account of that night's scamper that we learn the rebellion was abortive. Caught by the Linton's dog, she was taken into the Grange and magically transformed into an adult. Heathcliff tries to follow her ('Nelly make me decent, I'm going to be good') but is frustrated, and decides instead to be bad.[2]

[1] Kettle, *op. cit.*

[2] Thomas A. Vogler, *op. cit.*

Child/adult; bad/good; rebel/conformist. It all seems very simple. If we think of this 'transformation' in terms of the van Ghent approach, we could see it as an attempt by Catherine to become 'human'—that is civilized, socialized, adult. Heathcliff doesn't want her to grow up; he wants her to remain childlike and asocial; he wants to maintain their non-human 'natural' relationship.

Let's look more closely at the text. While Catherine is at Thrushcross Grange, Mrs Earnshaw visits her often—'trying to raise her self-respect with fine clothes and flattery' (p. 93). We have already seen Hindley demonstrating class-pretensions, in wanting to make certain changes in social relationship, separating 'family' from 'servants' (pp. 86–87), and he has already tried to keep Catherine and Heathcliff apart by emphasizing a difference of class. Now his wife tries to woo Catherine (with *fine clothes* and *flattery*) to become—not a socialized adult, or a civilized human—but a *lady*. 'You look like a lady now,' says Hindley (p. 93).

Catherine is a lady now in dress, manners and social attitudes. Her dress is now appropriate to the Grange rather than the Heights. Notice how 'she was obliged to hold up with both hands' 'a long cloth habit' (p. 93)—which suggests a very cumbersome and clumsy style of dress for a farmhouse. Her fingers are 'wonderfully whitened with doing nothing, and staying indoors'—she has become accustomed to a world where life is centred on the inside of houses; and where, above all, she *does no work*. She's become accustomed to a style of living where class-status and privilege place her above those who work for her, produce for her, and support her needs; and where her dress, and manners, and speech, and social attitudes, separate her absolutely from the inferior class.

The change goes deeper than that. In the first paragraph Nelly expects a 'hatless little savage' who would 'squeeze us all breathless'. Instead of demonstrative affection Catherine now shows passionless reserve. She dare not touch the dogs who come to 'welcome her', because they might dirty her clothes. She can't hug Nelly, she only 'kissed her gently', for the same reason. Most important of all, she has changed her attitude to Heathcliff. She still embraces him just as affectionately; but she sees matter for concern now in Heathcliff's dirty appearance.

> She gazed concernedly at the dusky fingers she held in her own, and also at her dress, which she feared had gained no embellishment from its contact with his.
>
> (p. 95)

Catherine thinks she can have everything that the other life can offer her—fine clothes, flattery, the status and privilege of a lady—and still retain the older relationship with Heathcliff. But Heathcliff refuses to take this lying down. How do you feel about Heathcliff's reactions?

> 'I shall not stand to be laughed at, I shall not bear it! . . . You needn't have touched me! . . . I shall be as dirty as I please, and I like to be dirty, and I will be dirty.'
>
> (p. 95)

Consider now the following questions in relation to this section and Chapters 6 and 7. Try and put something down in answer to all three questions.

(a) In Chapter 6, Heathcliff is the narrator of this description, our introduction to the Grange, and to Edgar and Isabella Linton. What reasons can you suggest for this? Would Lockwood have found the Grange any different? Does the narrative technique direct our attention in any way?

(b) Why is Heathcliff thrown out of the Grange, while Catherine is welcomed into the fold? Does the distinction that is made between them help you to understand (i) Heathcliff, (ii) the relationship between Catherine and Heathcliff?

(c) Heathcliff thinks Catherine will probably want to get out. She doesn't. What do you make of this?

4.3 'The eternal rocks beneath'

Please read Chapter 9 before reading this section.

This chapter is central to *Wuthering Heights* because it contains the fullest definition of the relationship between Catherine and Heathcliff, which is probably the heart of the novel. The most important passage in this chapter is that on pages 117–120, where Catherine gives Nelly reasons for her choice of Edgar rather than Heathcliff, and tries to define precisely the nature and quality of her feelings for Heathcliff. But I want you also to consider how the specific statement is built into the structure of the whole chapter.

Again I think that the narrative technique in this chapter is worth attention. This time Nelly is the person who interprets Catherine's experience for us, just as Lockwood does in the first chapters. I think we have to decide on how much we value Nelly's version of what happens, before we can value the happenings themselves.

The chapter begins with the scene (pp. 114–116) in which Hindley comes home drunk and accidentally almost kills Hareton. After Hindley has retired, Nelly sits down in front of the fire to rock the baby to sleep. The song that she sings:

> 'It was far in the night, and the bairnies grat,
> The mither beneath the mools heard that,'

refers to an old folk-belief that a dead mother could be disturbed in the grave by the sound of her babies crying. The song is, of course, appropriate to the child Hareton, because his mother is dead, and he is helplessly at the mercy of the brutal and drunken Hindley. Nelly, in *mothering* the child, is demonstrating an aspect of her personality which is emphasized throughout the novel.

The baby is present throughout the whole chapter, and his presence affects our response, has a special contribution to our sense of what is happening. Hareton is obviously in the middle of the initial scene, where Hindley's treatment of him is described in detail. Nelly tries to get him to sleep (p. 117); she refers to him sleeping (p. 120); Catherine takes him from Nelly (p. 121); and flings him on the settle when she goes out to look for Heathcliff (p. 123). Finally, Nelly takes the baby to bed with her (p. 126). I don't mean to say that the child is symbolic or metaphorical at all: he is simply present as a real force, a power for directing our feelings and attention where the author wants them to go. For example, we feel very strongly Hareton's vulnerability in the opening pages, which describe Hindley's drunken rage and affection. So we implicitly (perhaps unconsciously) *value* Nelly's protection of Hareton, the warmly maternal security she offers him. And I think this must affect our response to the conversation between Catherine and Nelly. I think we would be more inclined to respect, to feel sympathy for, to trust someone who looks after a child—far more than someone who drops it over a banister (Hindley) or 'flung' it on the settle to go and look for her boyfriend. Of course, Catherine is only a girl. But this contrast does underline things about Nelly, and things about Catherine too: that Nelly is conscious of certain basic values or moral forms (such as the way to bring up children) which other people in the novel ignore or pervert or (like Catherine) are oblivious of.

Read now page 117, 'Today, Edgar Linton has asked me to marry him', to the bottom of page 122; and consider the following questions. You should write notes on them in order to formulate answers in your mind: but they are intended to make you *think* about the passage, and I'd like you to bear them in mind as you read the rest of the novel.

(a) Examine the grounds for Catherine's choice of Edgar rather than Heathcliff. What do you think of them and where does Nelly stand in this debate?

(b) Nelly thinks that her 'catechism' of Catherine was 'not injudicious'. Do you agree? Do you think Nelly understands Catherine's predicament perfectly?

(c) Are you inclined to *agree* with Nelly's comments on Catherine's experience, or not?

The other issue that I want you to consider carefully is the exact nature of the love between Catherine and Heathcliff. You'll find the passage on page 122 ('Nelly, I *am* Heathcliff') discussed in most writings about *Wuthering Heights*, with what probably seems a bewildering variety of interpretations. Below I suggest some of the different possible ways of looking at it. By studying the passage in the light of these different views, I hope you will evolve your own sense of what it means. That sense will be part of your personal response to the novel: and that is something that can't be dogmatized, or insisted upon, or enforced; because it will depend not only on what the novel is like, but to some extent on what *you* are like as well. I don't mean that reading a novel is entirely subjective, a matter of every reader 'doing his own thing' and seeing what he wants to see. On the contrary: a great novel will probably act upon the reader, enter his consciousness and possibly change it; modify his attitudes, question his values, assault his complacency. But this process is a personal one, a relationship between the reader and what he is reading. And it's also important, in trying to think and write about the experience of reading a novel, that you should get the experience right, and not get too far away from it, to bend and distort and falsify. This means always sticking close to the text; substantiating ideas from the text; and keeping your *criticism* close to your *experience*.

Below are four different ways of seeing the love between Catherine and Heathcliff. I have not mediated at all between these different views, but have tried to argue for each one as eloquently as possible (my mother always said I should go into politics).

A.

'Ah me!
I am not thine; I am[a] part of *thee.*'
(Shelley)

In radio programme (2) *The Shadow of Scott*, Arnold Kettle talked about

Emily Brontë's relationship with Scott. This is just one of the connections between *Wuthering Heights* and the Romantic movement of the late eighteenth and early nineteenth centuries. In that talk you heard about Emily Brontë's use of certain familiar Romantic images, such as the child and the Byronic hero. Those of you who took the *Age of Revolution* course will probably find other typically Romantic features in the novel—the use of landscape, the connection of nature with emotional moods and moral values, the use of dreams, the use of the supernatural, and of effects which could be described as Gothic.

Most important is the emphasis on intense *feeling*, in the form of love and passion, which is fundamental to Romanticism. The quotation above from Shelley suggests how usual this kind of declaration of intense feeling was in Romantic literature—this sense of identification with the beloved. We can see here how *Wuthering Heights* became the Hollywood film of the same name. The love of Catherine and Heathcliff is romantic because it is intense, passionate and absolute. It is everything that love generally is *not* in ordinary life. In life we love, and cherish, often till death us do part: but we don't embrace on misty mountain tops, or sing Leibestods, or drink poison out of the same cup. In life passion exists, not in a simple and refined form, but inextricably involved with all the other aspects of relationship, and with the day-to-day material realities of ordinary life. The pure devotion of Catherine and Heathcliff fascinates us because it's something we can't often achieve, and can certainly never sustain. It is a form of escapism.'

B. 'My learned friend A is entitled to his opinion. But I would like to remind him that the Romantic movement was not merely a literary movement, but an *historical* one: and that an emphasis on intense feeling is something that emerged from a process of social change, and from a society which was working to dehumanize or destroy or pervert natural relationship and natural feeling. A novelist writing in such a society would naturally place a high premium on feeling and relationship. As Raymond Williams says:

The world we need to remember if we are to see these connections of the 1840s is the world of Blake: a world of desire and hunger, of rebellion and of pallid convention: the terms of desire and fulfilment and the terms of oppression and deprivation profoundly connected in a single dimension of experience.

Nobody later achieves Blake's kind of unity; he could only barely maintain it himself. But I think we need to start from the feeling, the central feeling, that an intensity of desire is as much a response, a deciding response, to the human crisis of that time as the more obviously recognisable political radicalism. Indeed, to give that kind of value to human longing and need, to that absolute emphasis on commitment to another, the absolute love of the being of another, is to clash as sharply with the emerging system, the emerging priorities, as in any assault on material poverty. What was at issue really was relationship itself: a dimension of relationship made problematic and dangerous by the increasing pressure, the external and internal and continuing pressure, to reshape, to deform—it is how Blake saw it—this most human, most absolute experience.[1]

Besides, there is nothing Romantic at all about Catherine's love. It is a familiar aspect of ordinary human experience.

These words of Cathy have been called mystical, or a romantic extravagance. But I don't know how that can be said if we listen and follow the action. That kind of bond, that sense of absolute presence, absolute existence in another, in

[1] Raymond Williams, *The English Novel from Dickens to Lawrence*, Chatto & Windus, 1970.

one another, is indeed an ordinary though of course always a transforming experience. In many lives, again and again, it is the central reality of everything else that happens, and indeed quite often doesn't need to be emphasised: the reality of the relationship is simply there and unbreakable.'[1]

C. 'I must protest that the two preceding gentlemen have got it all wrong. The most important thing about the love of Catherine and Heathcliff is that it is not *Romantic* or *historical*, but *religious*. "Surely you and everybody have a notion that there is, or should be an existence of yours beyond you" says Catherine. Their relationship is one of the soul, a spiritual relationship. It is therefore as *eternal* as the rocks beneath because it transcends time and material existence. All flesh is grass; flowers and foliage and Edgar Lintons fade, but the love of Catherine and Heathcliff endureth for ever'.

Like so many pairs of romantic lovers Catherine and Heathcliff are, so to speak, consecrated one to another, each feeling his or her passion as the consuming reality of existence. What is undeniably personal, however, in the manner of their love is the peculiar, almost religious intensity with which it is expressed and which perhaps finds its most significant manifestation in Catherine's attempt to explain her feelings to Nelly Dean.

The nature of Emily Brontë's experience of life, here perhaps expressed more directly than elsewhere, was religious in type; religious not merely in the sense of the rather indefinite 'mysticism' which has often been conceded to her on the strength of isolated passages in her poems, but in an awareness, at once more clear-cut and more open to definition, of the necessary incompleteness of all the elements that go to make up human nature in its time-conditioned state.[2]

D. 'The arguments of A, B and C all suffer from the same misconception—that the love of Catherine and Heathcliff is a kind of human love. It is in fact *non-human*. *Wuthering Heights* is a book irrelevant to the social and moral reason: the attitude to life implicit in it is rather one of "awed contemplation of an unregenerate universe than a feeling for values and disvalues in types of human intercourse". Heathcliff is an elemental figure, presented naked of civilized habits and ways of thinking, occupying an equivocal status on the edge of the human.

'The passions in *Wuthering Heights* are too simple, too undeviating in intensity to find an echo in practical social reality. Catherine and Heathcliff are not adult "characters": the complex attendant motivations of adult life, the recognition of the domestic and social responsibilities, the spiritual complexities of adult life are all lacking. They are in fact portions of the flux of nature, trying to identify themselves as human, but disrupting life by their appetite for an inhuman kind of intercourse. A possible form of relationship for them would have to be asocial, amoral, savagely irresponsible. They become caught in the economic forms of social life—Catherine in marriage and Heathcliff in property relations—but their passion is always inhuman, the desire to lose the self in otherness. In Catherine and Heathcliff the regressive desire is pure, and opens up the prospect of disintegration into childhood unconsciousness or death—that is, into anonymous natural energy.'

[1] *Op. cit.*
[2] Derek Traversi, 'The Brontë Sisters and Wuthering Heights', *Wuthering Heights:—A Collection of Critical Essays*, ed. Miriam Allott, Macmillan Casebook Series, 1970.

D is, of course, a summary of Dorothy van Ghent's essay in the Course Reader. Don't worry if you don't follow the whole of that, as it's a difficult essay and you'll understand it better when you have read the whole novel. But I think you'll gather from that summary how she sees the love of Catherine and Heathcliff.

You may find these differing views illuminating. You may find them merely confusing, and that would be understandable. The thing to do now is to sort out what *you* think about this matter. Does that love seem to you 'escapist'; or 'religious'; or 'a normal part of everyday experience'; or a 'non-human form of intercourse'? Don't think of these different attitudes as mutually exclusive—or as in any way exhausting the possibilities of response. The answer might be a combination of different views, or different from any of them. And the main thing to remember is that the 'answer' is not an absolute and definitive 'solution' to the problem—the answer will be your answer, formed by your own experience of reading the novel.

So now go ahead and read it.

PART TWO

The second part of the Study Guide consists of information about the novel, and about the novelist. It will not be profitable to read the former until you have completed your reading of *Wuthering Heights*. The latter (Section 4) can be read at any time, preferably before viewing the television programme.

The contents of Part Two are as follows: 1, Publication of the Novel; 2, Reception of the Novel; 3, A Note on Textual Accuracy; 4, The Novelist.

Ann, Emily and Charlotte Brontë, by P. B. Brontë (National Portrait Gallery)

1 PUBLICATION OF THE NOVEL

The three Brontë sisters, Charlotte, Emily and Anne, made their first attempt at publication with a joint volume of *Poems*, published pseudonymously in May 1846 (it appeared under the names of Currer, Ellis and Acton Bell, which the sisters also used for their novels). The *Poems* sold only two copies, but the sisters weren't disappointed, and were already engaged in writing novels. It is thought that Emily began *Wuthering Heights* in late 1845, and it was completed by summer 1846. The manuscript was sent, together with Charlotte's *The Professor* and Anne's *Agnes Grey*, to go the round of London publishers. In summer 1847 a publisher called Thomas Newby accepted *Wuthering Heights* and *Agnes Grey*, but rejected *The Professor*. Newby, more a commercial opportunist than a friend to literature, bumbled and vacillated over the printing until the immediate success of Charlotte's *Jane Eyre* (published in October 1847 by another company) made him realize he was on to a good thing. Two months later Newby published both novels in a three-volume edition, with *Wuthering Heights* by Ellis Bell in two volumes, and *Agnes Grey* by Acton Bell making up the third.

The success of *Jane Eyre* made the name of Bell an object of interest among the reading public; and Newby hastened to exploit the situation by confusing the identities of the three writers. He advertized *Wuthering Heights* in January 1848 as 'Acton Bell's successful new novel'. In February 1848 he again advertized *Wuthering Heights* as 'by the successful new novelist'—attempting to connect it with the very successful *Jane Eyre*. At one point he told an American publisher that 'Acton's new novel' (i.e. Anne Brontë's *The Tenant of Wildfell Hall*) was by the author of *Jane Eyre*, and that the same writer was responsible for all the novels. Newby may have been in some real confusion about the identities of the three sisters, but it's more likely that he deliberately encouraged mystification to boost sales. And as a sales promotion gimmick it worked very well. After both Anne and Emily had died, in 1850, Charlotte's publisher George Smith bought the publication rights from Newby, and published a one-volume memorial edition of *Wuthering Heights* and *Agnes Grey*. This was edited by Charlotte, and contained the Biographical Notice (Penguin edition, page 30) in which she tried to clear up the mystery of their identities, and which stimulated interest in the novels by including information about the strange and fascinating lives of the Brontës. In 1857 Elizabeth Gaskell published her *Life of Charlotte Brontë* and established the almost mythical Brontë legend—that fascination with the lives and works of the sisters which has persisted ever since, and which has (as I hope to show) been responsible for so much distortion, falsification, and misrepresentation of their achievement.

2 RECEPTION OF THE NOVEL

(Before reading this section, please glance again at Unit 2, pages 19–21.)

Throughout the first half of the nineteenth century, the novel was growing in status as a literary form: from being regarded as primarily entertainment, to being regarded as something like a serious art-form. Kathleen Tillotson in *Novels of the Eighteen-Forties*[1] has shown that this growth

[1] Kathleen Tillotson, *Novels of the Eighteen-Forties*, Oxford University Press, 1954.

in respectability can be seen in the literary journals of the time: where in the 1840s, the style of novel-reviewing gradually changed from the unambitious kind of review which simply printed long passages from the book under consideration, possibly praising it as a 'good story'; to more general considerations of the novel as an art-form. Of course, critics had taken novels seriously before, but there were no general assumptions to that effect among readers. Both these points are illustrated by Scott's review of Jane Austen's *Emma* (*Novelists on the Novel*, page 63)[1]: where Scott, fully aware of the value of what he has before him, nevertheless felt it necessary to insist that the novel is *not* 'beneath the sober consideration of a critic'. By 1821, reviewing Jane Austen's *Persuasion* and *Northanger Abbey*, the critic Richard Whately could express the opinion that 'the time seems to be past when an apology was requisite from reviewers for condescending to notice a novel'. He felt that this change was due 'not so much to alterations in public taste as to the character of the productions in question'.

Exercise

But what sort of 'seriousness' would be required of a novel in 1820, or in the 1840s? Look for a moment at two short pieces in *Novelists on the Novel*: from Daniel Defoe's *Colonel Jack* (p. 89) and Henry Fielding's *Tom Jones* (p. 91). How do these two writers try to justify the 'seriousness' of their productions?

Specimen Answer

By insisting that novels are really didactic, that they celebrate or exemplify principles of orthodox morality, and that they have a beneficial effect on the moral sensibility of the reader.

Exercise

Now look at the passage from Henry James' Preface to *Portrait of a Lady* (*Novelists on the Novel*, page 99). What is the big difference between James and Defoe?

Specimen Answer

Defoe thinks it's more important for a novel to be moral than to be true. Whether Colonel Jack's story is true or not doesn't matter, as long as the effect of the story is not immoral—as long as virtue is seen to be rewarded and vice punished. Henry James thinks the opposite: 'the question about it that disposes of all others—is it valid, in a word is it genuine, is it sincere, the result of some direct impression or perception of life? . . .' and he talks about 'the perfect dependence of the "moral" sense of a work of art on the amount of felt life concerned in producing it'. The novel's faithful representation of life is more important to James than its moral orthodoxy. D. H. Lawrence says much the same thing in a piece you have already read: *Morality and the Novel*. (See Unit 1 pages 25–26.)

[1] M. Allott, *Novelists on the Novel*, Routledge & Kegan Paul, 1959, (set book).

I wouldn't like to mislead you about these eighteenth-century novelists, who weren't by any means as simple-minded as this might suggest. In both these quotations, they are (I think) having their readers on—since the novels themselves aren't really moral tracts at all. Still, the fact that they could talk about (and play upon) these general attitudes indicates that they existed: and they are what we are interested in.

Two hundred years or so separate Defoe from James and Lawrence, two hundred years of social, literary and human change: during which time novels justified themselves as art to readers and critics alike. But one can see from the reviews of *Wuthering Heights* that the belief in the novel as didactic fiction was still going strong in the 1840s and 1850s. Critics and reviewers were divided about *Wuthering Heights*: some saw it as a radically immoral book; others saw it in terms of orthodox Christian or conventional morality, arguing that Heathcliff is presented clearly by Emily Brontë for our moral judgement and inevitable moral repudiation. Notice that whichever view they held, critics were generally agreed about what the moral character and function of the novel ought to be.

This novel contains, undoubtedly powerful writing, and yet it seems to be thrown away. We want to know the object of a fiction. Once people were content with a crude collection of mysteries. Now they desire to know why the mysteries are revealed. Do they teach mankind to avoid one course and take another? Do they dissect any portion of existing society, exhibiting together its weak and strong points? If these questions were asked regarding *Wuthering Heights* there could not be an affirmative answer given.

Tate's Edinburgh Magazine, February 1848

What may be the moral which the author wished the reader to deduce from the work it is difficult to say, and we refrain from assigning any, because, to speak honestly, we have discovered none. . . . There seems to us great power in the book, but it is a purposeless power.

Douglas Jerrold's Weekly Newspaper, 15 January 1848

Whether it is right or advisable to create beings like Heathcliff I do not know: I scarcely think it is. But this I know: the writer who possesses the creative gift owns something of which he is not always master—something that, at times, strangely wills and works for itself. He may lay down rules and principles, and to rules and principles it will perhaps for years lie in subjection; and then without any warning of revolt, there comes a time when it will no longer consent to 'harrow the valleys, and be bound in a band with the furrow'.

Charlotte Brontë (1850 Preface)

These critics all felt that *Wuthering Heights* was immoral. Others found it morally satisfactory. Charlotte was (characteristically) divided on this issue.

Heathcliff . . . is an incarnation of evil qualities; implacable hate, ingratitude, cruelty, falsehood, selfishness, and revenge. . . . If this book be the first work of its author, we hope that he will produce a second, . . . looking steadily at human life, under all its moods, for those pictures of the passions that he may desire to sketch for our public benefit.

Examiner, 8 January 1848

If the book have any moral it serves to show how fierce, how inhuman a passion personal attachment to another may become, and how reckless of the welfare of its object.

National Review, July 1857

The story shows the brutalising influence of unchecked passion. His characters are a commentary on the truth that there is no tyranny in the world like that which thoughts of evil exercise in the daring and reckless breast.

Britannia, 15 January 1848

Heathcliff . . . never once swerving in his arrow-straight course to perdition . . .

Charlotte Brontë (1850 Preface)

Generally the novels of Charlotte and Anne were found more palatable because they could be fitted easily into the category of didactic fiction. *Agnes Grey* was said to have 'an advantage over its predecessor [i.e. *Wuthering Heights*], that while its language is less ambitious and less repulsive, it fills the mind with a lasting picture of love and happiness succeeding to scorn and affliction, and teaches us to put every trust in a supreme wisdom and goodness' (*New Monthly Magazine*, 52, January 1848). Even *Jane Eyre* could be seen by a ladies' magazine *La Belle Assemblée* as 'a warning to all placed in authority over the young, whether in the capacity of parent, teacher or nurse . . . a warning against leaving the young and impressible to the charge of uneducated and lax-principled servants'.[1] But at least one reviewer, Elizabeth Rigby, in the *Quarterly Review* for December 1848, lumped both *Jane Eyre* and *Wuthering Heights* together, and went much further than a diagnosis of unprincipled morality:

Altogether the autobiography of *Jane Eyre* is a pre-eminently anti-Christian composition. There is throughout it a murmuring against the comforts of the rich and privations of the poor, which, as far as each individual is concerned, is a murmuring against God's appointment—there is a proud and perpetual assertion of the rights of man, for which we find no authority in either God's word or God's providence—there is that pervading tone of ungodly discontent which is at once the most prominent and the most subtle evil which the law and the pulpit, which all civilised society in fact has at the present day to contend with. We do not hesitate to say that the tone of mind and thought which has overthrown authority and violated every code human and divine abroad, and has fostered Chartism and rebellion at home, is the same which has also written *Jane Eyre*.

Wuthering Heights was even worse: 'too odiously and abominably pagan to appeal to the most vitiated class of English readers'. 1848 was a 'year of revolutions'; the February Revolution which overthrew the constitutional monarchy in France; revolutions all over Europe, in Italy, Hungary, South Germany; the crisis of Chartism in England; the publication of the *Manifesto of the Communist Party* by Marx and Engels. So the Brontë sisters had a lot to answer for. We'll return to that review.

[1] See Inga-Stina Ewbank: *Their Proper Sphere, The Brontës as Female Novelists*, E. Arnold, 1966, Chapter One.

3 A NOTE ON TEXTUAL ACCURACY

You should be reading *Wuthering Heights* in the Penguin edition, edited by David Daiches (1965). The Penguin text is to be greatly preferred to the copy you may have dug up from a bookcase or cupboard or out of the fluff under the bed. Apart from containing a very useful introduction and notes, it bases its text on the First Edition of 1847: whereas most editions follow the text of 1850, published by Charlotte Brontë after Emily's death. First editions have an importance to literary studies beyond their value as collector's pieces: because if the publication was supervised by the author, it represents the nearest we can get to what he actually wrote. Reprints and subsequent editions make many mistakes, and often severely distort the original text. In Chapter X of *Great Expectations* a messenger from Magwitch introduces himself to Pip by producing a file, which causes Pip to say: 'I knew that he knew my convict'. Carelessly edited texts have been printed which reproduce this sentence as 'I knew that he *was* my convict'; although it's only a matter of one word, the sense is completely altered.

'Textual criticism', the branch of literary studies concerned with establishing as accurately as possible what the author did write, is often treated lightly or slightingly by students and teachers alike, because of its concentration on boring details and pedantic minutiae. But clearly in a case like this, textual accuracy is of the first importance. With *Wuthering Heights* the textual situation is even more complicated. It was first published in three volumes in 1847, together with *Agnes Grey* by Anne Brontë in 1850 (both novels were shorter than the conventional 'three-decker' size). After both Emily and Anne had died Charlotte published a revised text with a Preface and Biographical Notice (Penguin edition, pages 30–41). She made extensive alterations to the punctuation and paragraphing of *Wuthering Heights*, and in case this seems to you a trivial matter, look at what Charlotte did to the last paragraph: in the 1847 text it stood as follows:

'I lingered round them under that benign sky; watched the moths fluttering among the heath and harebells; listened to the soft wind breathing through the grass; and wondered how anyone could ever imagine unquiet slumbers, for the sleepers in that quiet earth.'

Charlotte altered the punctuation so that in the 1850 text (and most subsequent editions) it reads:

'I lingered round them, under that benign sky; watched the moths fluttering among the heath and harebells, listened to the soft wind breathing through the grass, and wondered how any one could ever imagine unquiet slumbers for the sleepers in that quiet earth.'

This slight alteration which only changes the pauses after each clause, nevertheless alters the rhythm, movement and tone of this passage: and obviously in reading a novel which has been described as a dramatic poem in prose, we need to know precisely what the writer intended to say. But this isn't all Charlotte did: her relatively conventional mind failed in some ways to understand either her sister or her sister's novel, and felt vaguely disapproving about both. She went through *Wuthering Heights* trying to soften the tone here and there, to make it more respectable, less offensive to the sensitive ears of the Victorian reading public. In many places where Emily used vulgar or dialect words and idioms, Charlotte toned them down into respectable middle-class

Haworth Parsonage (Haworth Parsonage Museum)

speech, reducing the offensively vernacular expression to a more refined kind of language. At one point she substituted 'Hush, Isabella' for 'Give over!' 'To get her dinner upstairs' became 'to dine upstairs'. 'They became thick again'—'thick', an old popular word meaning 'close together', which has the very expressive concrete quality, close to metaphor, of much working-class speech—is rendered by Charlotte as 'friendly' or 'intimate'.[1]

I think the importance of textual accuracy varies from work to work and according to the reader's needs; one could argue that an academic writing a critical book needs an accurate text more than his student who is reading the book in a library, on a bus or in the bath, and trying to understand it on a less technical level. But now you know that a deliberate attempt was made by Charlotte Brontë to alter the character of *Wuthering Heights* (however slightly) by textual changes, to attempt to reduce the down-to-earth reality and the concrete texture of the language to a more urbane, more genteel, more standard middle-class kind of English, you'll appreciate the desirability of reading Emily's original words, in the Penguin English Library edition. (See also 'A Note on the Text', Penguin edition, page 369.)

[1] See David Wilson: 'Emily Brontë: First of the Moderns' in *Modern Quarterly, Miscellany*, No. 1, 1947.

4 THE NOVELIST

The Brontë's father, Patrick, was born Patrick O'Brunty or O'Prunty, the son of a peasant in Co. Down, Northern Ireland, in 1777. His home was a whitewashed shack some twenty feet square. Many Irishmen left their peasant homes to emigrate to England during this period, and went to work in the mills and factories of English cities, forming the poorest section of the slum population in towns like Manchester, Liverpool and London. Patrick was different: by 1802 (nobody knows how) he was at Cambridge University, where he took a degree and was ordained. He had a curacy in Yorkshire by 1809; married in 1812; and his wife bore their four literary children, Charlotte (b. 1816), Branwell (1817), Emily Jane (1818), Anne (1820). There were also two older daughters, who died young. The Rev. Patrick was appointed to the incumbency of Haworth in Yorkshire in 1820: he had risen rapidly from a barefoot Irish peasant to a respectable Anglican clergyman.

Rev. Patrick Brontë
(Brontë Society, photograph by Walter Scott, Bradford)

Haworth was not the remote and isolated country village which figures in the 'Brontë legend'. It was a big industrial village near Keighley, in the industrial West Riding of Yorkshire, near the centre of the woollen area; a rapidly growing town, whose population between 1811 and 1831 went from 3,971 to 5,835. There was nothing 'out of touch' about Haworth Parsonage: there couldn't possibly have been, since one of the most rapidly developing areas of industrial England was on its doorstep. The children inherited their father's interest in politics, and spent much time in political discussion. When the *Leeds Mercury* printed a series of letters from Richard Oastler about child labour in the worsted mills, the paper went to the Parsonage, and Charlotte may have read it. In any case, when she came to write about factories in her novel

Shirley she didn't have to go as far as Bradford for material—there were worsted mills in Haworth as well.

The Brontës grew up in the second, and in many ways the most important, phase of the industrial revolution. It was not the age of the primary inventions, of the first introduction of power-driven machinery and of the factory system, but rather of the consolidation and victory of that system, of the development of full-scale capitalism with its accompanying cycle of boom and slump and of continuous and intense class-conflict. Early in the century came the Luddite riots: there followed in succession the Radical agitation of the Peterloo period, the struggle around the Reform Bill of 1832, the growth of Trade Unionism in the early '30s, the fight for improved factory conditions and against the Poor Law of 1834, and finally the Chartist movement from 1838 to 1848. In every one of these, the West-Riding was a storm-centre.[1]

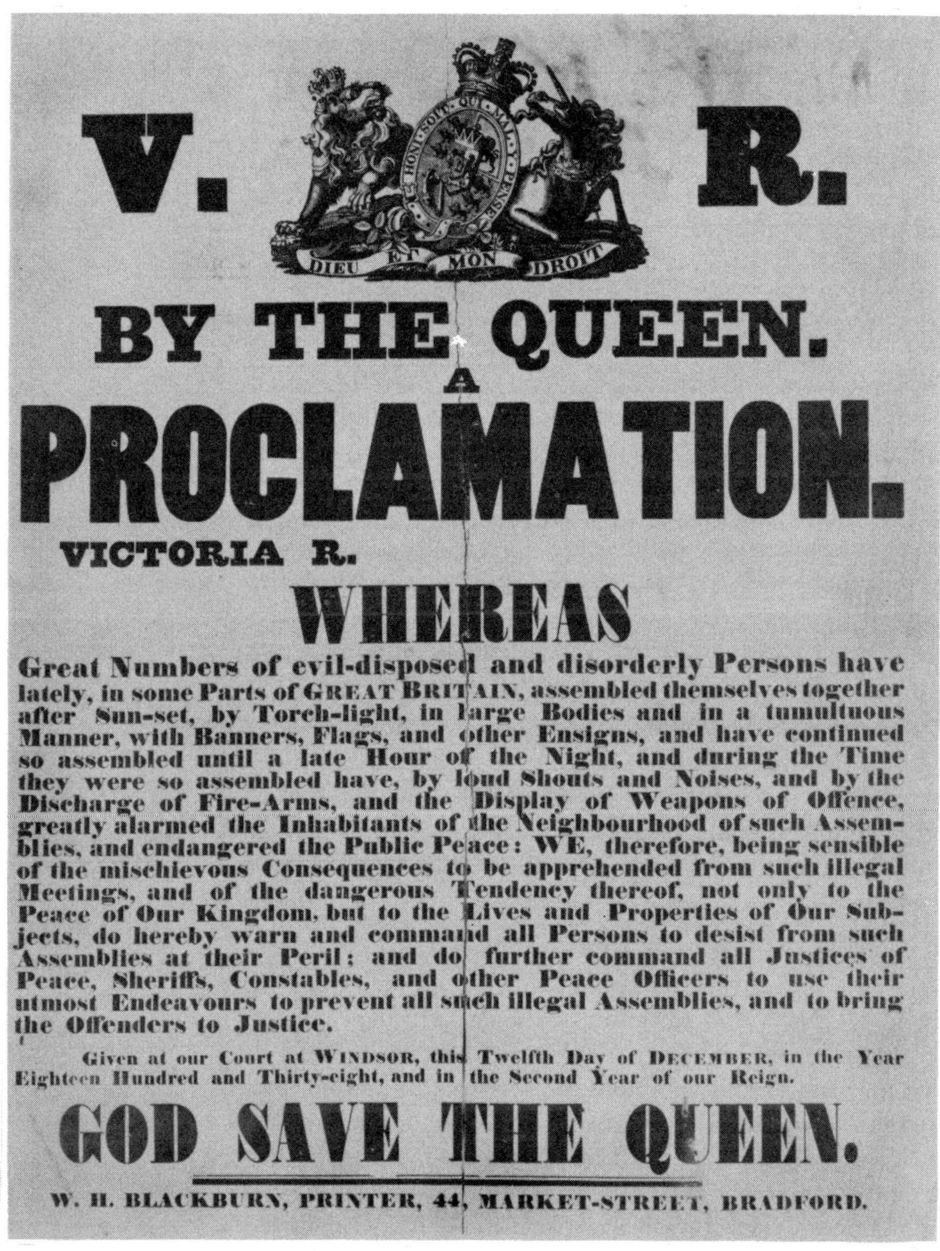

V. R.

DIEU ET MON DROIT

BY THE QUEEN.

A

PROCLAMATION.

VICTORIA R.

WHEREAS

Great Numbers of evil-disposed and disorderly Persons have lately, in some Parts of GREAT BRITAIN, assembled themselves together after Sun-set, by Torch-light, in large Bodies and in a tumultuous Manner, with Banners, Flags, and other Ensigns, and have continued so assembled until a late Hour of the Night, and during the Time they were so assembled have, by loud Shouts and Noises, and by the Discharge of Fire-Arms, and the Display of Weapons of Offence, greatly alarmed the Inhabitants of the Neighbourhood of such Assemblies, and endangered the Public Peace: WE, therefore, being sensible of the mischievous Consequences to be apprehended from such illegal Meetings, and of the dangerous Tendency thereof, not only to the Peace of Our Kingdom, but to the Lives and Properties of Our Subjects, do hereby warn and command all Persons to desist from such Assemblies at their Peril; and do further command all Justices of Peace, Sheriffs, Constables, and other Peace Officers to use their utmost Endeavours to prevent all such illegal Assemblies, and to bring the Offenders to Justice.

Given at our Court at WINDSOR, this Twelfth Day of DECEMBER, in the Year Eighteen Hundred and Thirty-eight, and in the Second Year of our Reign.

GOD SAVE THE QUEEN.

W. H. BLACKBURN, PRINTER, 44, MARKET-STREET, BRADFORD.

Proclamation of 1838 (Haworth Parsonage Museum)

[1] A. L. Morton: 'Genius on the Border', in *The Matter of Britain: Essays in a Living Culture*, Lawrence & Wishart, 1966.

These events were too close to be missed or ignored: Patrick Brontë was, as a clergyman, actually involved in strikes and lock-outs, at one time (despite his Toryism) incurring the wrath of the local 'ratepayers' by assisting the locked-out workers of his parish. Charlotte and Emily weren't confined to Haworth, but went much to Bradford, Keighley, Leeds—for a short time to Brussels; they both went to a school at Halifax, a Chartist stronghold, and the scene of one of the most notable Poor Law riots. On Hartshead Moor, only a few miles away, one of the biggest Chartist torchlight rallies took place in 1838. Charlotte used her experience of these events in her novel *Shirley*; Emily didn't write about them directly, but none the less they constitute her milieu, her social world.[1]

Before reading further, please turn back to *Mansfield Park* Unit 2, and read pages 28–30, 'Biographical'.

The fathers of Jane Austen and Emily Brontë were both country parsons, occupying therefore the same social position. And yet the lives of the two women were completely different, and that difference is reflected in their novels.

To start with there is the difference of locality: on the one hand rural Hampshire, a feudal setting of village and country-house life; on the other Haworth Parsonage, standing between the wild Yorkshire moors and the industrial valleys below. The difference between Haworth Parsonage and Steventon (or Mansfield Park) parallels the difference between Wuthering Heights and Thrushcross Grange.

Even the similarity of social position is deceptive. Jane Austen's grandfather was a Master of Balliol: Paddy O'Prunty's father probably slept with his pig. Jane Austen's brothers all went into the Navy, two becoming respected admirals. Patrick Brontë had no 'interest', and when his son Branwell failed in his chosen career as an artist, he had to get a job as a railway booking-clerk at Bradford. Unlike Jane Austen and the ladies in her circle, all three Brontë sisters had to work for their living—to take posts as governesses in the homes of wealthy mill-owners, teaching their daughters ladies' accomplishments. They weren't of course 'working-class' in any generally accepted sense: their father had a respectable social status, and they were ladies (albeit rather provincial ones). Their friends were upper-middle class. But there was a kind of insecurity of tenure about their social status and class position. There was the fact of their father's shady origin. There was the ambiguous social position of the governess, who would be treated in a rich household as a servant, even if she were more educated and cultivated than the family were. The alcoholism and moral collapse of their brother Branwell could be seen as further evidence of their ambiguous social status: he lacked the strength of will that the sisters had, to 'make his way in life unassisted'.

In other words, the social experience of the Brontë sisters was completely different from Jane Austen's: and this is partly why they wrote such different novels. At the beginning of *Mansfield Park* Fanny is a social outsider: but she eventually becomes a representative of the real spiritual and moral values of Mansfield Park. When she visits her father's home at Portsmouth, Fanny (and Jane Austen) compare the two worlds of the novel, and make a conscious moral choice between them. If we compare this with Lockwood's first visit to Heathcliff at the beginning of Wuthering Heights, we can see that Emily isn't *behind* the representative of the superior class. In fact she really knows more about the social world of the Heights than Lockwood does—which is just the point. It

[1] David Wilson, *op. cit.*

seems to me that Emily Brontë offers her reader a similar choice between the Heights and Thrushcross Grange: but the answer isn't so clear-cut or decisive.

One further point: Arnold Kettle noted that in Jane Austen's social context it was quite normal to regard servants as not fully human, and certainly as not particularly interesting. Emily Brontë is prepared to let a servant—Nelly Dean—tell her story for her.

Exercise

Look again at Unit 1, pages 17–18. Refresh your memory about the exercise you did then, comparing the opening paragraphs of *Mansfield Park* and *Wuthering Heights*. Have you found anything in Section 5 that illuminates the contrast between the two writers in their use of language? (This will be discussed in Unit 5.)

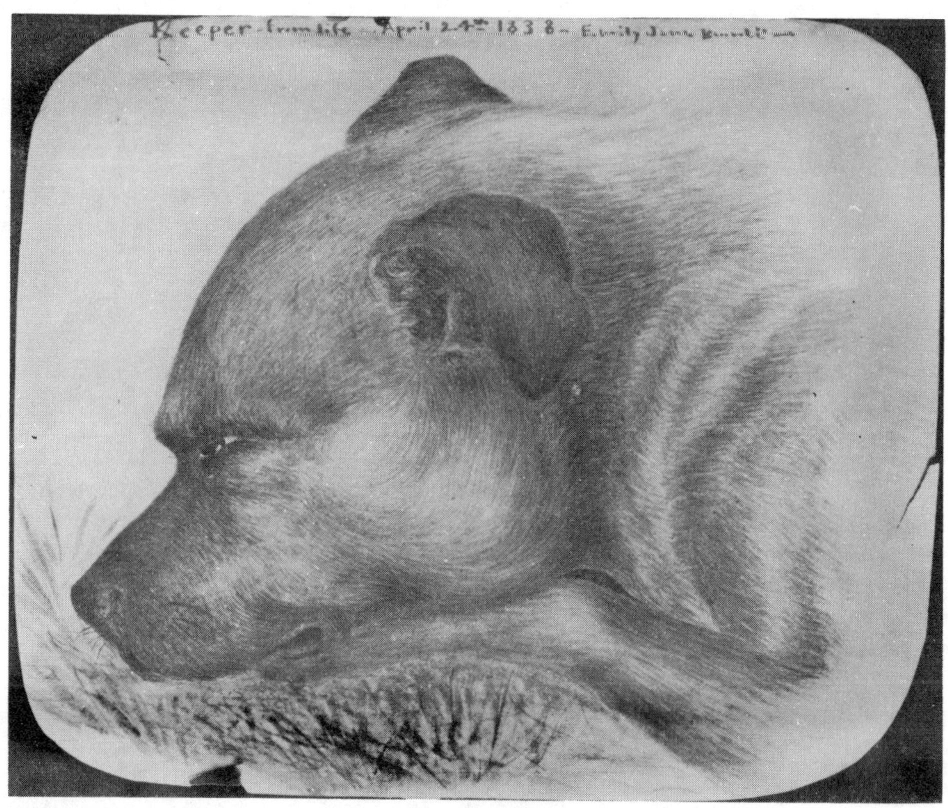

Sketch of Emily's dog, Keeper, by herself **(Haworth Parsonage Museum)**

I will close this section of the Guide by giving you two passages: one from a letter of Charlotte Brontë, the other a fragment of a Diary by Emily; with the object of suggesting something of the actual quality of life at Haworth Parsonage. (This is also partly the object of the related television programme.) Charlotte is here writing to her friend Ellen Nussey, and trying very hard to give the impression that the Brontës are perfectly model ladies, and spend their time in pursuits proper to ladies.

An account of one day is an account of all. In the morning, from 9 o'clock till half past twelve, I instruct my sisters and draw; then we walk till dinner time. After dinner I sew till tea-time, and after tea I either write, read, or do a little fancy work, or draw, as I please. Thus in one delightful, though monotonous course, my life is passed.[1]

[1] Quoted in Ruth H. Blackburn (ed.), *The Brontë Sisters: Selected Source Material*, D. C. Heath & Co., New York, 1964.

November the 24
1834 Monday
Emily Jane Bronte
Anne Brontë

I fed Rainbow, Diamond Snowflake Jasper pheasent (alias this morning Branwell went down to Mr Drivers and brought news that Sir Robert peel was going to be invited to stand for Leeds Anne and I have been peeling Apples for Charlotte to make an apple pudding and for Aunts [illegible] Charlotte said she made puddings perfectly she was of a quick but limited intellect Taby said just now Come Anne pillopatate (ie pill a potato Aunt has come into the Kitchen just now and said where are your feet Anne Anne answered [illegible] On the floor Aunt papa opened the parlour Door and [illegible] gave Branwell a letter saying here Branwell read this and show it to your Aunt and Charlotte — The Gondals are discovering the interior of Gaaldine Sally mosley is washing in the back Kitchin

A bit of lady [illegible] hair done by Anne

[illegible]

November the 24 1834

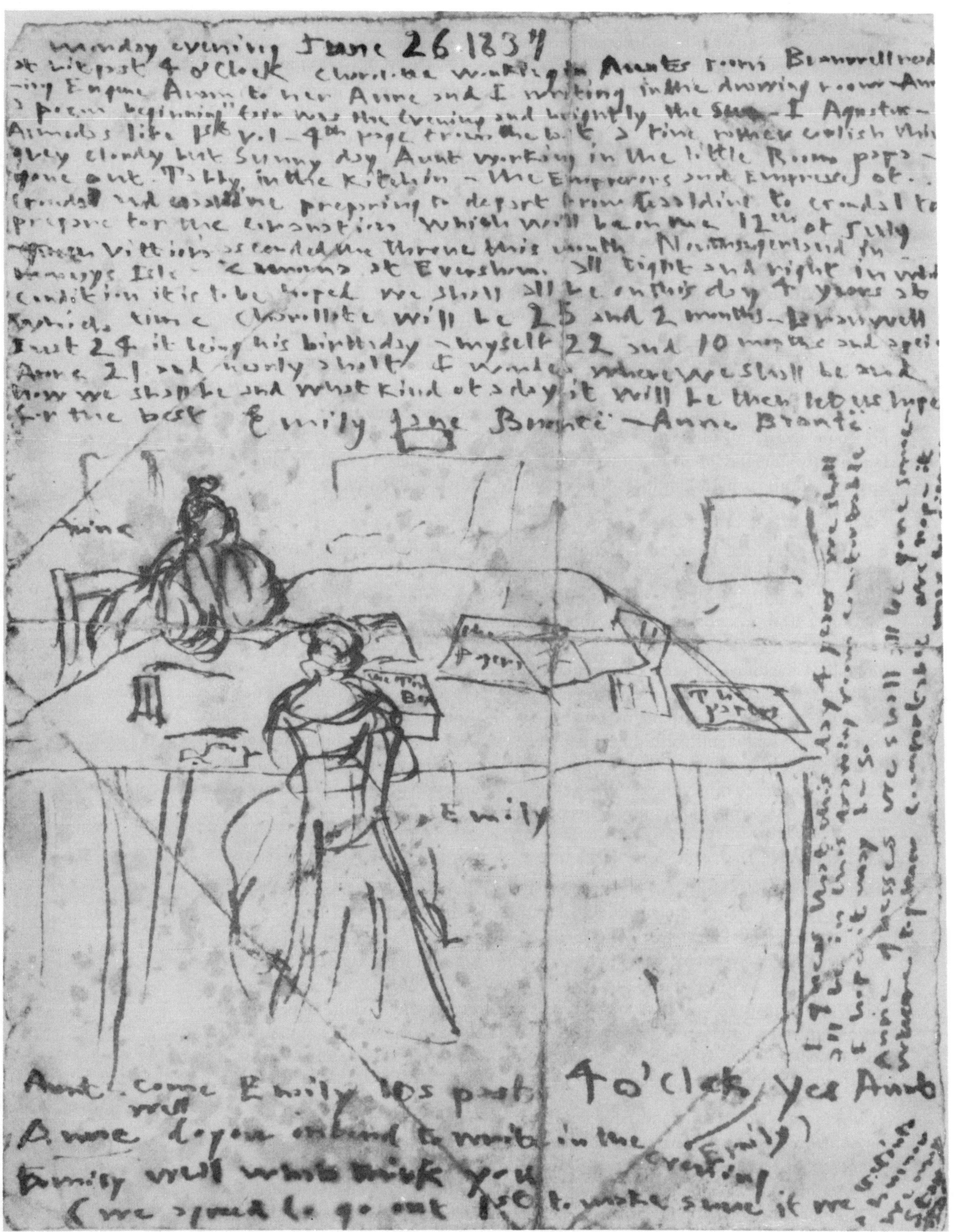
Monday evening June 26 1837

A bit past 4 o'Clock Charlotte working in Aunts room Branwell reading Eugene Aram to her Anne and I writing in the drawing room — Anne a poem beginning "Fair was the evening and brightly the sun — I Augustus — Almedas life 1st v. 1 — 4th page from the last a fine rather coolish thin grey cloudy but Sunny day Aunt working in the little Room papa — gone out. Tabby in the Kitchin — the Emperors and Empresses of Gondal and Gaaldine preparing to depart from Gaaldine to Gondal to prepare for the coronation which will be on the 12th of July Queen Vittiora ascended the throne this month Northangerland in Monkeys Isle — Zamorna at Evesham. all tight and right in which condition it is hoped we shall all be on this day 4 years at which time Charlotte will be 25 and 2 months — Branwell just 24 it being his birthday — myself 22 and 10 months and a peice Anne 21 and nearly a half I wonder where we shall be and how we shall be and what kind of a day it will be then let us hope for the best Emily Jane Brontë — Anne Brontë

Aunt. come Emily its past 4 o'Clock Yes Aunt

Anne well do you intend to write in the evening

Emily well what think you

(we agreed to go out 1st to make sure if we ...

Diary fragments, November 24th, 1834, and June 26th 1837, in Emily's handwriting (Haworth Parsonage Museum)

Charlotte here depicts the sisters like three of Jane Austen's ladies, without giving any indication of how different the Parsonage must have been from any normal respectable home. It was very small, with very small rooms; family and servants were close together all the time, and the servants on intimate terms with the daughters (see below); the sisters did housework as well as needlework, and the house must have been pretty noisy and active, as it was constantly full of tame animals—dogs, cats, two tame geese which lived in one of the ground-floor rooms, sheep, goats and anything else they picked up on the moors—not to mention Emily's tame hawk, Hero. But perhaps the most striking difference between Charlotte's account, and what was really going on, is suggested by this:

Many a bright eye lingered on his form and followed it as he passed. He regarded them too with a careless and condescending smile which brightened into flashing pride as his glance turned on the now departed multitude. . . . He seemed to be in the full bloom of youth; his figure was toweringly, overbearingly lofty, moulded in statute-like perfection, and invested with something which I cannot describe—something superb, impetuous, resistless, something in short no single word can altogether express. His hair was intensely black, curled luxuriantly, but the forehead underneath, instead of having the swarthy tinge appropriate to such Italian locks, looked white and smooth as ivory.

My Angria and the Angrians

This is the Duke of Zamorna—a character from Charlotte's fantasy world of Angria, but based on the actual Duke of Wellington. While Charlotte was drawing, walking, sewing and having tea, her imagination was also at work. All four Brontës wrote volumes and volumes of these fantasy romances: Charlotte and Branwell creating the world of Angria, Emily and Anne that of Gondal. Charlotte obviously felt that awareness of their imaginative lives shouldn't be shown in public, or even admitted to full consciousness. Look now at a piece of the autobiographical Diary by Emily. This I think conveys much more vividly and truthfully the texture and movement of Brontë life. Of course this was a private Diary paper, not a letter to another person: Emily needed to have no inhibitions. (She was simply unprepared to compromise on this point: she wrote hardly any letters at all.)

I fed Rainbow, Diamond, Snowflake, Jasper pheasant

This morning Branwell went down to Mr Driver's and brought news that Sir Robert Peel was going to be invited to stand for Leeds. Anne and I have been peeling apples for Charlotte to make an apple pudding. . . . Tabby [their servant Tabitha Ackroyd] said just now Come Anne pilloputate (i.e. peel a potatoe) Aunt has just come into the kitchin and said Where are your feet Anne Anne answered on the floor Aunt. Papa opened the parlour door and gave Branwell a letter saying Here Branwell read this and show it to your Aunt and Charlotte. The Gondals are discovering the interior of Gaaldine. Sally Mosley is washing in the back kitchin.

It is past 12 o'clock Anne and I have not tidied ourselves, done our bed work, or done our lessons and we want to go out to play We are going to have for dinner Boiled Beef, Turnips, potatoes and apple pudding The kitchin is in a very untidy state Anne and I have not done our music exercise which consists of b major Tabby said on my putting a pen in her face Ya pitter pottering there instead of pilling a potatoe. I answered O Dear, O Dear, O Dear I will directly With that I get up, take a knife and begin pilling.

Emily's Diary Paper, November 24 1834[1]

[1] Quoted in Ruth H. Blackburn (ed.) *op. cit.*

Recommended Reading

You should read in any case the essay 'On *Wuthering Heights*' by Dorothy van Ghent in the Course Reader: Arnold Kettle (ed.), *The Nineteenth-century Novel; Critical Essays and Documents*, Heinemann Educational/Open University Press, 1972; and David Daiches' *Introduction* to the Penguin edition of *Wuthering Heights*. The following books and critical pieces are also recommended:

Allott, M. (ed.) *Wuthering Heights, a Collection of Critical Essays*, Macmillan, Casebook Series, 1970.

Ewbank, I., *Their Proper Sphere: The Brontës as Female Novelists*, E. Arnold, 1966.
Kettle, A., 'Wuthering Heights' *Introduction to the English Novel*, Hutchinson 1951 (paperback).

Other essays which you might find interesting are:

Cecil, D., 'Wuthering Heights', *Early Victorian Novelists*, Constable, 1934, (paperback).

Klingopolous, G. D., '*Wuthering Heights:* the Novel as a Dramatic Poem', *Scrutiny*, XIV, 1947.

Leavis, F. R. and Leavis, Q. D., 'A Fresh Approach to Wuthering Heights', *Lectures in America*, Chatto & Windus, 1969 (paperback).

Morton, A. L., 'Genius on the Border', *The Matter of Britain: Essays in a Living Culture*, Lawrence & Wishart, 1966.

If you want to read about Emily Brontë's life (the subject of the television programme), read Winifred Gérin: *Emily Brontë*, Oxford University Press, 1972.

Acknowledgements

Grateful acknowledgement is made to the following for illustrations used in this unit:

Brontë Society and Walter Scott; Haworth Parsonage Museum; National Portrait Gallery.

NOTES

The Nineteenth-century Novel and its Legacy

1 General I: Introduction
2 *Mansfield Park* Study Guide
3 *Mansfield Park*
4 *Wuthering Heights* Study Guide
5 *Wuthering Heights*
6 *Great Expectations* Study Guide
7 *Great Expectations*
8, 9 *Cousin Bette*
10, 11 *On the Eve*
12 General II
13, 14, 15 *Middlemarch*
16, 17 *What Maisie Knew*
18, 19 *Jude the Obscure*
20 *Huckleberry Finn*
21, 22 *Germinal*
23 General III
24, 25, 26 *Anna Karenina*
27 Joseph Conrad
28 E. M. Forster
29 D. H. Lawrence
30 Virginia Woolf
31 James Joyce
32 General IV